IMPACTFUL
Online Meetings

How to Run Polished Virtual Working Sessions
That are Engaging and Effective

Zoom|Webex|GoToMeeting|Skype|Google
Hangouts

Printed in the United States of America

ISBN 978-1-7344153-3-9 (eBook)

ISBN 978-1-7344153-4-6 (Paperback)

First Edition

14 13 12 11 10 / 10 9 8 7 6 5 4 3 2 1

Contents

Important Note

Register Your Copy of this Book for Additional Content, Notifications of Book Updates and Access to

FREE VIDEO TRAINING

Go to: ImpactfulOnlineMeetings.com

This book was part way through completion when the US was hit with the COVID-19 pandemic. We rushed to get it to market because it was clear that a huge number of companies were asking employees to work remotely and that the number of online meetings was going to increase exponentially. We knew the information we had was going to be very valuable to people looking for help navigating this new situation.

While there is a great amount of useful content in this book, we will also be expanding and polishing it in the coming weeks.

One of the great things about the eBook platforms is that we can update this book at any time, and you, the reader, can get that update without paying again. Your eBook store (such as Amazon) sometimes will "push" updates, but often they don't. However, you can force the book to update if you know there is new material.

That is why we highly recommend you add your email to the book mailing list at ImpactfulOnlineMeetings.com. This will allow us to alert you when we update the book as well as let you know about free videos or other tools that we create to supplement the book. If you are reading this book in printed form, if we add significant new material to the book we will make a PDF supplement available to print purchasers. Future enhancements such as this will be announced via the mailing list.

Introduction

Meetings are the heartbeat of business. They are where information is shared, ideas are generated, decisions are made, and work is coordinated. That's why the effectiveness of meetings can make or break a company.

With the introduction of more flexible workdays and increasing opportunities to "work remote", more and more meetings are "going digital." The convenience and other advantages of web conferencing software are undeniable, and during the current pandemic, they have become a necessity for employee health.

But running an effective online meeting is different from doing so in-person, and that's why many are run sub optimally. According to the Harvard Business Review, a correctly run virtual session can be even more effective than an in-person meeting. But most meeting leaders lack the full knowledge to do so. This book aims to correct that.

Co-authors, Howard Tiersky, CEO of FROM, the digital transformation agency, and Heidi Wisbach, SVP of Business Innovation for FROM, have been leading virtual teams and facilitating online working sessions for Fortune 1000 companies for more than ten years. FROM runs Innovation Loft, NYC's most creative team collaboration facility, where Howard and Heidi have developed a wide range of techniques to teach groups to energetically engage around knowledge sharing, problem solving, and decision making.

In this book, Howard and Heidi lay out many little-known tips for making the best use of online conferencing software, keeping online attendees engaged, facilitating discussion amongst large groups, making the best use of visual material when presenting online, and other formerly undocumented techniques. You can use this information to run fantastically successful online meetings for groups of four to 400 or more.

CHAPTER 1

The Importance of Online Meetings

There are a lot of benefits to replacing in-person meetings with webinars, but it also creates challenges. Executives, managers and facilitators who run virtual meetings need some distinct skills in order to lead them professionally. This book will provide you the information you need to plan and host online working sessions that are not only far better than 99% of those that people participate in today, but that in some ways can exceed the effectiveness of in-person meetings.

The Importance of Meeting Effectiveness

It is estimated that in the US alone there are over 11 million meetings held every single day. According to studies by MIT, the average employee spends at least six hours per week in meetings, and mid- to senior-level managers can spend as much as half of their working time participating in meetings.

All this time spent in meetings is expensive. If six employees, earning an average of $60,000 per year, each meet for an hour, the cost for that meeting in salaries alone is around $350. If we do that 11 million times a year, it means that just in the US we are spending almost $4 billion a year on meeting time. And that doesn't even include the cost of the donuts!

A survey of 1000 US and UK professionals found that with the average conference call running 38 minutes, an average of 15 minutes is wasted getting started and dealing with distractions throughout. All these lost minutes equate to billions of lost dollars.

Another study showed that employees estimate that the percentage of meetings that are literally of "no value" is approximately 37%, suggesting that we are wasting as much as $1.5 billion per year on worthless meetings. That doesn't even factor in all the meetings that aren't totally worthless, but have only marginal value.

And meetings are critical to the success of companies. They are one of the primary ways we share information, come up with ideas, make decisions, coordinate our work activities, and create relationships. Companies whose meetings are "above average" in their effectiveness can expect to see a significant impact to their overall productivity and success.

Meetings are "Going Digital"

While face-to-face meetings still play an essential role in business, every year a larger and larger percentage of meetings are done as webinars.

1. Our global economy means teams are increasingly decentralized, so critical meetings often require participation of people who aren't based in the same office.
2. The cost of office space in many urban areas has skyrocketed. To reduce these costs, as well as to create more flexible work-life balance, companies are becoming more virtual, with more employees working from home.
3. As a result of reducing office footprints, even for those working *in* the office, at many facilities conference rooms are in high demand and not always available.
4. Many companies have tightened up their travel budgets, reducing the opportunity to travel to attend meetings.

Furthermore, many companies recognize that for business continuity preparedness, it's important that their teams have the skills and experience in collaborating remotely because it could be necessary at any time—whether due to a weather incident such as a hurricane or blizzard, a facility issue such as a heating failure or fire, or other disruptive incidents such as threats or acts of terrorism, epidemics or riots. The cost of business "stopping" in such circumstances is too great to risk, so teams must be prepared to continue operating even if they cannot be co-located for a period of time.

For these reasons, companies are shifting more and more meetings into the digital realm. A ZDNet study estimated that employees in the US spend nearly three billion hours a year in some form of virtual meeting and Fortune estimates that the global video conferencing market will grow at a rate of around 10% a year for the next six years.

A Lot of Virtual Meetings are Bad

A delightful viral video made the rounds a few years ago satirizing company conference calls and the awkwardness and inefficiency that often occurs: constant dings with people arriving and departing, difficulty hearing people, social weirdness, problems with access codes, distracting background noises and notifications, AV that doesn't work, people first trying to talk simultaneously and then simultaneously saying "go ahead," followed by awkward pauses, etc.

We've made this video available on the home page of the book website at ImpactfulOnlineMeetings.com if you want to check it out (and there are a variety of

other templates and tools there as well, so it
worthwhile resource to bookmark).

This video has been viewed more than 16 million
times on YouTube alone, so it clearly resonates with
the experience of many living the corporate lifestyle.
Clearly there are some challenges associated with both
the technology and the way conference calls, web-
meetings, or hybrid meetings are run.

It Doesn't Have to Be that Way

The good news is that it doesn't have to be that
way. According to *The Harvard Business Review*, online
meetings can be *even more effective* than in-person
meetings when done right. But how many people have
really been *trained* to run an effective online meeting?
Running effective *online* meetings is typically outside
of school or company training agendas.

At our company, we provide training for leaders of
online meetings to empower them to not just make
them less painful and awkward, but to make them
truly outstanding. We actually started out focusing on
running highly impactful *live* workshop sessions, and
we still do this for a large number of Fortune 1000
clients at our facility, the Innovation Loft in New York
City. However, we found over time that for the
reasons stated above, more and more companies were
asking us to do some of those working sessions online.

Years ago, when these requests started coming in, we initially balked. We believed firmly in the value of in-person interaction, especially for full or multi-day working sessions, and we tried to discourage clients from moving them online. But our clients were persistent and we started to experiment with the format. What we discovered was that we were able to adapt many of the techniques that made our live sessions so incredibly engaging and productive to online work. Along the way we have expanded our toolbox of digital tools and techniques to bring clients to a whole new level of online meeting engagement, and now enthusiastically share them through articles, this book, and our in-depth video training series. .

You may be interested in conducting large-scale virtual workshops with 50 or more people that last anywhere from a half day to several days, as we do, but you may simply want to run your six-person staff meeting more effectively, or somewhere in between. In any of these scenarios, the principles in this book are designed to help you. We are also augmenting this book with tutorial videos, tip sheets and other materials available on the book website at ImpactfulOnlineMeetings.com.

CHAPTER 2

When to Hold an Online Meeting

Online Meetings vs In-Person Meetings

In the prior chapter, we talked about the challenges with online meetings in corporate America today. However, it should be acknowledged that in-person meetings are no panacea. Many live meetings lack clear purpose and direction, go on too long, allow some participants to filibuster, or subject participants to "Death by PowerPoint."

So, online meetings are not entirely unique in their challenges. Many of the same core principles of meeting success apply. However, there are a variety of differences that need to be taken into account for success.

In this book we will provide a formula for success in online meetings, including both those components that overlap with running a live meeting as well as those which are specific to virtual sessions.

In our experience, there are pros and cons to any meeting format, and one of the first things you need to determine is whether a given meeting *should* be online or not (or frankly, whether it needs to occur at all). Let's take a look first at some of the pros and cons of online meetings and then we'll dive into some of the key practices in order to make them successful.

What's Great About Online Meetings

In the olden days, the only way to "meet" was to ensure everyone was in the same location. This meant that jobs that involved frequent meetings generally required employees to be full time in the office. It required travel time and expense to get participation from those based in other locations. It meant that if you had several meetings back to back, you needed to allow time to get from one to the next, even if they were just on different floors of the same building. It meant that if there wasn't a conference room available, you might not be able to meet at the preferred time. It also meant that if an employee was late, sick, or otherwise unable to arrive at the designated physical location, either they missed the meeting or the meeting had to be postponed.

Once upon a time, these didn't even seem like problems because they were obvious, necessary requirements for meetings.

Eventually, it became possible for a lone participant to be "piped in" to a meeting via conference phone, but that was usually an awkward experience— trying to follow a live session with only the audio to go by. It was hard to tell who was speaking and sometimes even to hear, and there was no access to visual aids. So if someone remembered you were on the phone, they'd need to say something like, "Bob is showing his forecast charts now. They look amazing. Sorry you can't see them."

Then came conference calling bridges in the 90's, followed more recently by web conferencing software like Zoom, Webex, and GoToMeeting. These tools allow meetings to occur virtually with participants dialing or logging in from anywhere in the world. They provide some supremely useful features such as:

- The ability to share screens to show PowerPoints, spreadsheets, software demos, etc.
- Displaying the name of who is speaking at the moment.
- The ability to chat with participants via text.
- The ability to use your device's camera to show your face (or other physical items) to the other participants.

And, depending on the conferencing platform, they can permit voting, virtual breakouts, call recording, even real-time subtitles of the call for those in quiet environments or who are hearing impaired.

It cannot be denied that there are some pretty useful things that can be done in a virtual meeting that weren't possible in a traditional in-person meeting. In addition, of course, the very nature of digital meetings offers flexibility you can't get with in-person meetings as they free participants from needing to be in the same place and from needing to book a conference room. Plus you save money on sandwiches.

What is Lost with Online Meetings

Online meetings also have some drawbacks. A lot of this book addresses ways to *overcome* the potential downsides to online meetings, such as participants being distracted, low engagement, and technical issues which may create barriers to full participation. These barriers can be overcome using the techniques we will outline.

However, it's important to realize that there are also *inherent* limitations of virtual sessions that suggest that *some* meetings are better held in person if at all possible. Here are some areas where in-person meetings are generally superior.

Establishing Relationships

There is no denying that relationships are more effectively *established* via in-person interactions. In this book we will provide a variety of techniques to *improve* this, however today there is no full replacement for the value of shaking someone's hand, looking them in the eye, and having a meal together.

Physical Experience

Second, sometimes there are physical requirements of a meeting that are difficult or even impossible to fully simulate digitally.

For example, we recently facilitated a workshop for a large sports league as they planned an upcoming championship game at a specific sports stadium. The ability for the participants to walk through the facility was invaluable and never could have been done by Webex effectively.

Similarly, sometimes there is an object or set of objects that are critical to the meeting, like a prototype of a new type of toaster or a samples of the new flavor of soft drink that your company will be marketing. The opportunity to touch, smell, and taste things cannot be replicated online—at least not yet.

Emotional Moments

Sometimes there are things that just need to be said in person. News of layoffs, mergers, or celebrations of success are much more effective live. And there are times where sensitive negotiating and hashing through complex, politically-charged issues requires the opportunity for close reads on eye contact and body language. While video calls are certainly far better than audio only, something important is still lost compared to being face to face with team members at emotional moments.

With these limitations in mind, you need to determine whether a given meeting is "right" for an online format. In our experience, 90% of meetings can still work very well virtually. Just look out for the 10% that are worth the time, effort and expense to hold in person.

Making sure certain key meetings *are* held in person is actually a key contributing success factor for having outstanding *online* meetings.

For example, once we had *done* the stadium walkthrough and project team members had that shared reference point, subsequent virtual meetings to discuss the plans were very effective.

Similarly, once people have *established* relationships in person, digital interactions can be very effective at further developing them, and their collaboration online will be far richer because they feel they are dealing with a real human being, not just someone they know "online."

This is one of the reasons why we facilitate so many full and multi-day in-person workshops for teams, which include a great deal of team building. We find that teams that work remotely *most* of the time can massively improve the effectiveness of their *online* interactions through infrequent but intensive in-person interaction.

Or Do You Even Need a Meeting?

I often joke that my favorite type of meeting is a *cancelled* meeting. Isn't it a joy when you see that space open up on your calendar and you think about all the productive or enjoyable things you can now do with the time? They say you can always earn more money, but there's no way to get any more *time*, so there's no greater gift than someone giving you an hour of your life back.

That's not to say we should go ahead and cancel all our meetings. As we've said before, meetings are the heartbeat of a company...but if the heart is beating *too* frequently, that's called an arrhythmia and you need to see a doctor immediately.

During intense workouts—or intense projects— you may need that heart to beat more frequently. At other times it's better to relax, meditate, and let the rhythm be slower.

In future chapters, we will talk about how to clearly define the purpose of a meeting and from there, ascertain its appropriate duration, participants, and so on. As part of that process, you should certainly ask whether there is a clear goal for the meeting. If not, perhaps the meeting is unnecessary.

And even if there is a clear goal, ask yourself, is a meeting the best or only way of accomplishing it? Can it be done via an email? Or a shared brainstorming document? We are big believers in having great meetings, but one way of having great meetings is to use the tool called "meetings" when it's needed—when "real time" interaction is required.

When participants build trust that you will use their time wisely and have meetings only when needed, they'll be more eager to click "Accept" to your invites.

CHAPTER 3

The Formula for a Successful Online Meeting

What Are You Trying to Achieve?

Any business activity, such as a meeting, must have a purpose. So why do we have meetings? While most meetings have multiple purposes, in our experience meeting leaders often don't think through the specific purpose in a deliberate manner, which decreases their effectiveness. Just like anything else we undertake, we can't know if we were successful if we don't know what we were trying to achieve.

In general, most meetings are held for some combination of five categories of objectives.

1. Sharing Information

You need to update a group of people with announcements, project status, or other information.

In some cases, the purpose of the information may be to support other meeting activities, such as brainstorming, and in other cases it's just information participants need to do their job, such as a new policy they need to follow.

While there are other ways to share information, there are multiple benefits of sharing information in meeting format.

1. You know who was there so you know who received the information.
2. You can communicate more effectively using your voice and body language than, for example, in an email or memo.
3. You can "read the room" to gauge participants' reaction.
4. You can take questions.

These four benefits together can often equate to the difference between information being effectively shared or not, so meetings can be a very valuable format for information sharing.

2. Coming Up with Solutions (or Validating Them)

The classic "brainstorming" meeting brings team members together to utilize their experience and creativity to try to identify different possible approaches to achieving a goal, whether it's rebranding the company or planning the holiday party. Some meetings may be exclusively for this purpose, but it's also common for an agenda item in a meeting that also has other objectives to include discussion about how best to solve a given problem.

3. Making Decisions

Many executive meetings involve agenda items that require a decision, whether that's a formal vote or simply the search for consensus. It may be a budget allocation decision, a personnel decision, a decision on a product launch or marketing campaign, or any one of a wide range of other decisions that must be made to keep a business running.

4. Coordinating Activities

Many business processes require multiple teams to work together to achieve a result. Meetings often occur to enable individuals or teams to explain how they intend to proceed and coordinate their plans, schedules, resource needs, or other requirements with colleagues.

5. Socialization

Lastly, one purpose of meetings that should not be overlooked is building social bonds. Many studies show that teams who have warmer and more knowledgeable personal relationships work better together.

A meeting may be *exclusively* for socialization purposes, such as the classic "meet and greet," but more often it's just one benefit of meeting, but one that meeting leaders should seek to achieve as often as possible.

So, whether your meeting is focused on trying to land a new account, conducting employee performance reviews, or kicking off a new project, most likely its objectives fall into these five categories of sharing knowledge, coming up with solutions, making decisions, coordinating activities and socialization. Furthermore, it's very common for meetings to have objectives that cover *all* of these areas in a single meeting.

It's helpful to keep this in mind so that as we start to look at the key steps to go through in planning an online meeting, we can map them back to how they support these different activities.

What Makes a GOOD Meeting?

If the five categories we just covered represent what you want to achieve, how will you know if you have done it well? What has to happen in a meeting for these to be successful? Here are five key characteristics to any good meeting.

Mindset

The number one characteristic of a great meeting is the mindset of the participants, including the leader. Have you been in meetings where you were bored, didn't want to be there, or were resentful that your time was being wasted? How effective were you in those meetings?

These days many people will "multitask," even during an *in-person* meeting where others can observe their behavior. And if that's what they do *in person,* what do you think they are doing when they can't be seen in an online meeting?

By the way, brain scientists tell us that the human brain is actually not capable of true multitasking.

Multitasking by humans really just means switching back and forth between activities—or to put it more bluntly, ignoring one thing while doing another. So let's just call multitasking what it is: people tuning out during your meeting.

In a survey we did, 85% of respondents admitted to "regularly" checking emails and surfing the web during conference calls.

And what about the other 15%? We're not sure, but our research team hypothesizes that they probably lie about other things as well.

In contrast, have you participated in sessions where you were excited and engaged? How much did you contribute? How impactful was *that* meeting in influencing you?

Having participants on the edge of their seats, looking forward to what comes next and seeking an opportunity to participate makes a 10,000% difference in the effectiveness of a meeting.

Now you may be thinking, "Please, this is a *conference call*, a web meeting...nobody is going to be on the edge of their seats!" Well, reset your expectations. It's more than possible—we'll show you how.

Purpose

We started with "mindset" because many of the other keys to success inter-relate with our mindset goals, such as defining a clear *purpose* to a meeting.

Successful meetings have a clear purpose defined for them. This is true even if a meeting is recurring. The leader should consider before each *individual* meeting, "What is the purpose of *today's* meeting?" There are several reasons why this is critical.

First, for mindset. When participants know that they are there for a *reason* and they have a goal to achieve, then there is the potential for victory. Their time can be spent achieving something. In contrast, if it feels like the meeting is just a ritual or an opportunity for the boss to sound off, their mindsets are likely to be poor.

Second, in order to be able to declare an online meeting a success, we have to know what the finish line is. A meeting that achieves nothing is clearly not a success.

And a meeting that achieves *something* may or may not be a success. That can only be gauged against the meeting's goals.

If the goal of the meeting is to decide on next season's product line-up, but what we accomplish during the meeting is actually learning about Angela's problems with her boyfriend and giving her advice on how to deal with him, well that was "something" accomplished, but it's hard to call it a success (and that guy's really not right for Angela anyway).

And even if the time is spent on what appears to be a productive business purpose, for example discussing the features of an awesome new product put out by our competitor, well, it may have been good to share that information, but we didn't achieve our goals, and now we're even further behind the eight ball as we still have no product line-up and everyone is depressed about the company's future.

A well thought-out purpose helps keep us on track. When everyone in the room knows the definition of team success during the meeting, they are likely to remain on target. If it's not clear what the purpose is, it's tempting to just try to find *something* we can actually achieve during the allotted time that we can be proud of. The odds are, though, that if we are flailing around looking for a purpose during the meeting we probably aren't going to make very strategic choices.

Engagement

Engagement means full and active participation. It's the impact of "mindset" on the actual *behavior* of the participants. When participants are engaged, they listen attentively, they ask questions, they offer ideas, and they fully participate in whatever activities are part of the meeting.

Engagement also means they are engaging with their fellow meeting participants, which supports socialization goals.

We will talk at length in this book about specific techniques to get online meeting participants engaged.

Content

Most meetings involve some form of content, whether it's a presentation, bullet points to cover, sample ad campaigns, or documents to be discussed. The question is: what do meeting participants need in order to be successful and achieve the objectives of the meeting? Ensuring that content is available to the participants in a format where they can access and understand it is often critical to meeting objectives. In some cases, the understanding of the content may be a goal of the meeting and in other cases it may be a tool to support other objectives.

For example, if the goal of a meeting is to come up with ideas to solve the conflicts in the manufacturing schedule, then critical content probably includes the current schedule and information about what is causing the conflicts. If the information about schedule conflicts is fairly detailed, it may be most productive to provide in advance, since reviewing it is probably more of a solitary activity and meeting time is best used for activities that require group involvement. .

Often in meetings, content is *presented* by someone, whether the meeting leader, or another participant, or a guest. Making sure that presentation is interesting, relevant, and concise is also part of ensuring the success of the content component of a meeting. We'll talk more about how to do this later as well.

Ease

The last key characteristic of successful online meetings is ease, which is about ensuring that there are no obstacles to participation. This means scheduling the meeting at a time people can join, confirming the technology works, and making the necessary support resources available for anyone that needs help. It means having the meeting start and end on time and making sure that participants can see and hear clearly.

Conference calls and webinars have some common challenges in this area. We'll provide tips to overcome them in later chapters.

So that's the *goal*. If you are seeking to bring people together to share information, come up with solutions, make decisions, coordinate activities, and/or socialize, you *will* be successful if you:

1. Have a clear **purpose**
2. Get participants in the right **mindset**

3. Get them fully **engaged** behaviorally
4. Incorporate high-quality, digestible **content** aligned with the purpose
5. Make it **easy** to participate

But how can you *do* all of those things? That is what the rest of the book is going to cover, following this structure:

1. How to **plan** for an online meeting (Chapter 4)
2. How to ensure you get the **technology** right (Chapter 5)
3. How to effectively **present** and **facilitate** discussion (Chapter 6)
4. How to get **engagement** (Chapter 7)
5. And how to **follow up** after a meeting to maximize its impact (Chapter 8)

If you do all five of *these* things correctly, you can hit all of the keys to success we described earlier for any meeting.

Planning a Meeting

Not all plans are successful, but rare is the success that did not begin with a plan. Online meetings are no different. The number one reason online meetings fail is because there is not a sufficiently clear plan to support their success.

Planning an online meeting involves nine components:

1. Purpose
2. Agenda
3. Participants and Scheduling
4. Meeting Rules
5. Meeting Roles
6. Advance Communications
7. Content Creation and Preparation

8. Platform Settings
9. Testing & Rehearsal

Many of the items in this list may *seem* obvious, but before you skip this chapter saying, "I know all this stuff," here are two warnings.

First, while some of these may seem apparent, most meetings overlook at least one "obvious" preparation activity, so having a clear checklist is key.

Airplane pilots "know what they need to prepare," before starting their takeoff, but they still go through a *written* checklist before *every* flight just to be sure they don't forget something.

Second, in this chapter we have provided some tips and distinctions *about* some of these seemingly obvious categories, which you may not have heard before.

Defining the Purpose

As mentioned in the last chapter, the process of planning an effective meeting *must* start with a clear sense of the purpose and build from there.

We advocate breaking the purpose into three parts: the outcomes, the reasons, and the activities.

The Outcomes

The outcomes should be clear deliverables that you want to check off as "done" during the meeting.

They will likely fall into some or all of the five categories of meeting goals we defined in the last chapter. For example:

- To make sure everyone on the team understands the new tax policy
- To generate at least ten ideas for possible new accounting practices
- And to decide what day to release the client newsletter.

That's one communication objective, one solutioning objective, and one decision to be made.

Outcomes should be as *specific* as possible, and it should be very easy to tell at the end of the meeting whether or not they have been achieved.

That means outcomes are focused on *the meeting*, not the larger project. A meeting outcome cannot be "construct the best new skyscraper in the world," that is, unless you plan to build a skyscraper *during* the meeting. The outcome could certainly be to agree on which architect to hire.

The Reasons

"Reasons" are very powerful. They are the "why" *behind* the outcomes—why *achieving* the outcomes is important and beneficial.

For example, if your outcome is to make sure the team understands the new tax policy, the "why" might be, "so we don't get audited and have to work weekends for six months as a result," and also, "so we can save the company millions of dollars and all get our bonuses."

The "reasons" serve to help motivate the leader and the team to be engaged with achieving those outcomes.

Look for and communicate both "positive" reasons that participants can be excited to achieve the outcomes of the meeting as well as "negative" reasons—consequences that happen if the group fails to achieve the outcomes. If you have both types of reasons, the participants' motivation and attention will be twice as powerful.

The Activities

The activities simply define what you will seek to "get done" during the meeting in order to *achieve* the outcomes. For example, if the outcome is to make sure everyone understands the new tax policy, the activities related to that might be to review the PDF issued by the IRS, to brief them on some additional advice you got from your outside counsel, and then to answer any questions the team may have.

Although they are closely related, activities and outcomes are *not* the same. For example, could you go through those activities and *still* not achieve the outcome of ensuring everyone *understands* the new tax policy?

Well, if half the team is playing minesweeper during your online meeting, then of course you could!

When defining the components of the purpose—the outcomes, reasons, and activities—consider soliciting input in advance from prospective meeting participants. They may have thoughts about what the most important objectives for the meeting should be as well as *why* they are essential and what types of activities would most productively achieve those outcomes.

When participants have a role in shaping the purpose of a meeting, they are also more engaged from the start.

Agenda

Agendas are a sequential plan of what will occur during a meeting. Think of the agenda as the careful orchestration of activities each done for a specific reason to drive toward your desired outcome.

You should never begin building an agenda before you are clear on the purpose of the meeting, since clearly the only benefit of the agenda is to *achieve* the purpose of the meeting.

Using the process described above to define the meeting's purpose, including the activities, should give you a good sense of what needs to happen during the meeting. There are only three more decisions that need to be made to adapt that into an effective agenda: sequence, duration and owner.

Sequence

Defining the sequence of activities is often straightforward.

The very first item on any agenda should be a restatement of the purpose of the meeting, including the reason component, so participants understand and are reminded of the definition of victory by the end of the meeting as well as the reason why achieving it is worthwhile.

To start sequencing the rest of the meeting, start with dependencies. Clearly, if information needs to be communicated before a decision about it can be made, then that sequence is obvious.

But you may also have various independent activities to sequence that don't have inter-dependencies, and there may be more than one potential right answer for the sequence. Here are a few tips for deciding.

It can be valuable to begin with some quick socialization topics to get the group connected to each other. We have a PDF of some ice-breaker activities (some of which take less than one minute) on the book website.

Then consider what is likely to be on people minds coming into the meeting. If there are any "elephant in the room" topics, deal with those early or they will be a distraction.

For example, consider that if you are talking about defining big plans for the future, but participants are worried about how they'll get through the work they already have on their plates, you may need to give them a chance to clear them mind of current challenges before they can leap with you into to the future

On the other hand, if you have some sort of fun or exciting announcement, you may want to hold it for the end, letting the participants know that it is coming but keeping the outcome a surprise to create suspense. That's why they do the "Best Picture" award near the end of the Academy Awards, to make sure you keep watching.

It's great to start a meeting with a feeling of quick victory, so if you have some easy, rapid items that you expect will be non-controversial and quick to address, you may want to start with those.

If you have an agenda item that you think may be intense or create some conflictual discussion, it's best to put it in the middle—get people warmed up and feeling productive, and then hit the challenging topic. Leave something positive for the end to conclude on an upbeat note.

Meetings should end with a recap of what has been accomplished, as measured against the goals of the meeting. Ideally, you are illustrating that the group has been successful at achieving all of the goals of the meeting. If for some reason this is not the case, it's best to acknowledge it and propose an approach to complete the objectives (such as a follow-up meeting or other mechanism).

Duration

You need to determine both how long your overall meeting will be as well as how long each agenda item should be scheduled for. Most meetings are longer than they need to be, so seek to determine the shortest possible time in which the objectives can be achieved.

Long presentations can often be abbreviated when tested against a clear purpose. Is all that information necessary to achieve the goals? Or only some of it? Perhaps the rest can be provided as a pre-read or sent out afterwards.

You should usually allow time for questions and discussions, depending on your objectives. However, meeting discussion can also go on too long and spin in circles if it's unstructured. In the facilitation chapter of this book, we will discuss techniques for discussion acceleration which may enable you to schedule less time, while still encouraging participation.

Once you determine the duration needed for each individual activity, that should allow you to determine the total length the meeting needs to be.

If you find you have scheduled too much for the time that is available (such as during a regular recurrent meeting) then you may want to spread your objectives (and associated activities) over several meetings.

Also consider whether all of the objectives *need*
be addressed in a meeting. As discussed earlier, some
objectives may be able to be accomplished in more
efficient ways outside of the meeting.

Owner

Each part of the agenda should have an owner who
is responsible for the content and outcomes of that
section of the meeting. It could be that all the agenda
items of the meeting have a single owner; however, it
is often better for variety and optimal preparation if
there is some distributed ownership.

It's important for the meeting to have cohesion
and logical flow, so even with different owners for
different parts, the master owner of the meeting will
want to be aligned with each activity owner on the
goals, content, and format of his or her section. You
want to avoid redundancy or even contradictions
across sections of the meeting. Ideally, presenters look
like a coordinated team and not like a bunch of people
who all just showed up at the same time to present
something.

Participants and Scheduling

Meeting planning often begins with an assumption
of who the participants will be, but we believe this is
the wrong sequence.

As we've mentioned, there should be no meeting if there is not a purpose. Once the purpose is understood, including the activities, then a logical question is: who do we need there? If we are making a decision, who needs to be a part of that? If we are coming up with ideas, who would be a strong contributor, etc.? So remember to take the time to ask the question, "Who should be at this meeting?" "Who actually has the information, skills, and/or the authority we need to get things done?" Don't just assume it's "the usual folks."

If your meeting has multiple objectives (as is common), then it's useful to do this mapping for each objective to see whether some objectives call for different participants than others. It's difficult for participants to stay engaged for the full duration of a meeting if only part of it is relevant to them, not to mention it being a waste of their time.

So if you find you have significant diversity in terms of who needs to be a part of different activities planned for your meeting, consider whether you should really be planning several shorter meetings, each with the relevant stakeholders.

Once you've defined the duration and participants, then you have the challenge of scheduling it at a time when everyone can make it.

Tools like Outlook and Google Calendar are helpful for this when all the participants work for the same company because they will search out times when all of the proposed participants have free time on their schedule (if such a slot exists). If you have participants from different companies or other scheduling challenges, then you need someone "on point" to do the manual work of coordinating with participants to find a time that works.

If you have participants in many time zones, good tools to help check what cities/countries are in what time zones include Every Time Zone, World Clock Meeting Planner, and Worldtimebuddy.

Meeting Rules

Rules are a cornerstone of civilized society. Without them, there'd be traffic jams at every corner, businesses would have no way to ensure people paid their bills, and we'd have to fear for our lives every time we walked on the streets. It would be chaos.

Have you ever been in a meeting that felt kind of like that?

Rules are important to good meetings and it's far better if they are decided in advance. You may find that you have a set of "standing rules" for meetings within your organization. If so, that can be a great starting point, but if you don't, you may need to create them from scratch.

Furthermore, sometimes situational rules are needed for a given meeting. For example, perhaps you typically have five people in your weekly operations update meeting and everyone can provide feedback informally. But you have a special initiative underway, so you have invited ten additional people to the meeting. That may necessitate a little different set of operating rules for things to run smoothly.

One approach we will often take during virtual meetings with more than ten participants is to say that initial feedback on an idea should be entered into the chat tool in our conferencing platform. That way the presenter (or someone helping the presenter) can quickly scan 20+ pieces of feedback in really just a few seconds, notice patterns of commonality, respond to those items that merit discussion, or just take note of those that are fairly straightforward.

Situational rules like this are far better when planned and communicated in advance rather than implemented during a meeting once a problem becomes evident. If three people get to give verbal feedback and *then* the leader notices it's taking too long and asks the rest to enter theirs in the chat, they may feel slighted, impacting their mindset. You *should* do this on the fly if necessary, of course, but that's why planning is so important. You can make your meeting far more effective by anticipating these types of needs in advance.

What other types of rules should you set for your meetings? It does depend somewhat on the size of meetings, corporate culture, and other factors, but here are ten commonly effective rules which can work across a wide range of meeting types:

1. **Be on time.** It's very inefficient if meetings must hold for latecomers, and once you start to do that it becomes self perpetuating.
2. **Be there or send an empowered, informed delegate.** If you confirm attendance at a meeting, keep that commitment, or if something makes that impossible, have someone else there who can gather the information you need to know and respond on your behalf if decisions need to be made.
3. **Come prepared**. This is true both for presenters and participants. Being prepared for an online meeting means being at your device, in an appropriate environment, with good connectivity, and having reviewed any pre-reading material.
4. **No multitasking.** Let participants know you expect their full attention. In the chapter on "engagement," we will go into some tactics to both motivate this and test it.
5. **Cameras on**. Expect a 200%+ improvement in the effectiveness of online meetings if everyone has their cameras on, turning an audio call into a video conference. These days, most of your participants will have sufficient bandwidth, and nearly all computers have cameras, so any barriers are largely matters of habit. We'll talk more about this in upcoming chapters.
6. **Be succinct.** Franklin Roosevelt offered this advice to aspiring public speakers: "Be sincere, be brief, be seated." This works well in online meetings as well. It's good to remind presenters and participants providing feedback that they

will be appreciated for their ability to make their points with alacrity.

7. **Make commitments and follow through.** Many meetings ask participants to make some type of commitment to action. Attendees should be expected to bring the information they will need in order to make the anticipated types of commitments and then to follow through on the commitments they make in the meeting.

8. **Play full out.** Participants should fully engage with the meeting. That means being energetic, listening, taking notes, asking questions, and being candid when asked their opinion, among other behaviors. You can help them with this by running a great meeting using the principles in this book (many more to come).

9. **Be positive.** Feedback and discussion should stay positive in tone and be based on underlying respect for colleagues and presumption of goodwill. If genuine disputes arise, the rule should be "take it offline" from the meeting.

10. **Accept facilitation.** Help participants understand that the leader of the meeting has a tricky job—to make good use of everyone's time by not letting the meeting run too long, but also to achieve all the objectives and to be sure all key points are heard. That means that sometimes the facilitator may need to move things along or ask for conversations to be tabled (put in a "Parking Lot"). Participants should understand that when this request is made they should honor it in a positive way and move on.

Meeting Roles

One reason we see leaders of online meetings struggle is because they try to "do it all themselves." This is unnecessary. It's unreasonably difficult to try to present content, facilitate questions, ensure the meeting stays on time, check on the whereabouts of latecomers, take notes, and deal with any technical issues all at the same time.

It's *possible* for one person to try to wear all of these hats, but why? Usually there are others who can take on some of these responsibilities. Not only does it let the leader be more focused, but if some of these other roles are taken by other *participants* in the meeting, it makes them pay much closer attention.

I have five kids and have spent many a weekend day at their baseball, softball, soccer, lacrosse, and hockey games. Oh and also their swim meets, gymnastics competitions, track meets and wrestling matches.

At the risk of sounding like a bad parent, I must admit that I have often found it difficult to pay full attention to whatever game or competition I am attending, and my focus would often drift. Next thing you know I'd be checking my emails, my kid would score a goal, and I'd have missed it.

Then one day I was asked during one of my daughters' basketball games to run the scoreboard. The parent that usually did it wasn't there for some reason.

It's not difficult. You watch the game and then start and stop the timer when play starts or pauses and then push buttons to increment the score when they make a basket.

Well, once I was given that simple task, my attention was riveted on the game, because *I had a job to do.* I didn't miss a single basket or play that my kid was in during the whole game. You might think having this responsibility would have *distracted* me from the game, but in fact the opposite was true.

Here are some potential roles in a meeting. Either the leader must take them on, someone additional must be brought to the meeting to fill them, or they can be assigned to a participant, depending on circumstances. Seek to distribute responsibilities as widely as is practical.

1. **Facilitator**. Responsible for kicking off the meeting, running the agenda, keeping things on time. If you always facilitate your own staff meetings or other recurring meetings, consider letting others give it a try.
2. **Presenter**(s). Responsible for sharing specific units of content and possibly engaging in related discussion.
3. **Timekeeper.** Watches the clock to see how the meeting is progressing compared to schedule and *subtly* alerts the facilitator and presenters so they know how to adjust their speed and content.

4. **Note-taker.** Responsible for documenting the meeting—purpose, participants, agenda, action items and owners, decisions made, discussion points

5. **Expert resource.** While not always present, it can be fruitful to have people invited to the meeting because they have expertise in an area pertinent to the topic. They might be a presenter, but they might simply be present to answer questions if they come up.

6. **Presentation operator**. Some presenters prefer to have someone else advance slides or do whatever else is necessary to make the AV portion work correctly (play videos, run a demo, etc.)

7. **Participant support.** This role helps participants who have problems connecting or have questions about the conferencing software, and potentially reaches out to any late participants with a reminder that the event is starting. Or, this person can also help manage other interactive tools during the meeting, such as chat, polls, Q&A, and virtual breakout rooms. We'll be discussing many of these methods of engagement in future chapters (and we go into much more depth about them in our video training series).

Of course, this doesn't mean you need seven people to run a meeting. Different meetings will emphasize different types and levels of interaction and thus have different requirements. One person could try to fill all of these roles, or, for example, it's not uncommon for the leader to act as facilitator, expert resource, presenter, and presentation operator, with perhaps another person playing the other three roles.

But if the meeting has a number of participants, consider distributing these roles around. If you have a standing meeting, it can create worthwhile variety to rotate these roles to different members of the team for each meeting. Or, you may find someone "finds their home" with a particular role and wants to play it on an ongoing basis.

But above all, be sure all these roles are covered, any gaps run the risk of getting in the way of a smooth meeting.

Advance Communications

You can support participants being fully prepared for the meeting, in a great mindset, and ready to play by the rules by sharing the right advance communication.

Common formats for advance communication are email and calendar invites, but could also include announcements made at prior meetings and setting expectations for future meetings.

Good topics to include in communications include:

1. **Logistics**. Key logistics include date and time, webinar connection instructions (including international dial in numbers if applicable), physical location if one is available as an option, and any "acceptance" expected to gauge attendance.
2. **Purpose**. Restate the purpose, reasons, and, potentially the key activities. Be sure to include the "why." Think of your advance communications as "marketing" for the meeting. Why should participants not just come in an obligatory way, but look forward to the meeting as an important opportunity?
3. **Preparation**. What do participants need to do to be ready for the meeting? This might include pre-reading, a survey, material they need to bring with them such as budgets or sales figures, "pre-thinking" they may want to do to support idea generation, or technology they need to have participate (such as a good internet connection, downloading the web conferencing software, etc.). Encourage participants who are using an unfamiliar platform to test it before the start time of the meeting.
4. **Support**. Where should the participant turn if they need help in preparing for the meeting? Questions may surface about content, scheduling, technical connection support, or other topics and you'll want to have some way to triage these concerns. .
5. **Rules.** If the meeting is following pre-established "standard" rules, it's always good to

mention that and link to a central place where those rules are available. If there are any situationally-specific rules for this particular meeting, be sure to state those.

6. **Roles.** Be sure to let individuals who have specialized roles during the meeting, such as presenters or note-takers, know in advance what the expectations are. Give them time to prepare, especially if the role is unfamiliar.

Content Creation and Preparation

Part of your preparation will involve ensuring the content needed for the online meeting is prepared.

It may be that the content already exists in advance of planning the meeting and it's simply a question of making sure that either the files are sent out in advance or they are ready to be screen-shared by either the presenter or the person doing the presentation support. Make sure you have coordinated clearly *who* will be sharing the content from their screens. You don't want that moment in the call when you are having a conversation during the meeting about who has the files and who wants to share them. Figure that out in advance.

It's smart to preview any materials that will be screen shared to be sure they work well at their current format and size.

For example, we've seen presenters try to share Excel spreadsheets during an online meeting only to discover that zooming out makes the data illegible and zooming in loses the overall context.

In cases like this, adjustments may need to be made (such as reformatting, hiding columns, etc.) and this is best done in advance.

Depending on your circumstances, some participants may join via a smartphone and be looking at any shared documents on a rather small screen, so bear that in mind when designing slides. Keep them simple and the text size large or you risk them being unreadable on phones.

Also, be sure that the level of detail of the presentation materials matches the time allotted. It may be that there is a 40-slide deck, but if you only have 10 minutes allocated on the agenda, you can only cover certain key slides. These decisions should be made in advance, not "on the fly" during the meeting. However, it can still be beneficial to have the other slides easily accessible in case there is a question best answered with one of those omitted detail slides.

One last part of the "content" of the meeting will be any exercises or group activities that will be facilitated as part of the session, but we'll talk about those in the chapter on engagement.

Platform Settings

When a meeting is created in web conferencing software, there are a number of configuration settings, some of which are quite important to customize in order to optimize your meeting. Each platform is different and we won't attempt to cover all the settings your software may have, but here are some that are especially important to consider.

1. **Which account to use.** Most organizations will have multiple accounts on a given web conferencing platform. It's not necessarily important whose account is used as long as the meeting leader can gain "host" control to be sure the meeting is correctly started and to control the configuration.

   However, be careful not to have a meeting be scheduled "under" the account of someone who is not participating in the meeting because you may not be able to launch the meeting or, once in the meeting, you may not be able to access meeting controls.

   In addition, be careful about scheduling important online meetings back to back on the same account. You want to avoid a situation where one meeting runs over and either the participants in the second meeting receive the dreaded "Meeting cannot start because another meeting is in progress" message, or possibly worse, find themselves dumped into the end of an unrelated meeting. The best solution is to have enough accounts that you can leave some "breathing room" between scheduled meetings to allow for overrun as well as time for meeting hosts to join a little before the scheduled start time.

2. **Join before host**. This feature allows participants who arrive before the host to join the meeting. Some platforms will default this to "off," meaning it will not allow the meeting to "start" until the host has joined. Another similar feature is "Leave attendees in Waiting Room" which is often defaulted to "on". This puts participants in a virtual waiting room and, even if the host is indeed in the meeting, he/she has to admit each new attendee as they connect. The risk of these default settings is that if the host is delayed or has difficulties logging in, the entire meeting can be delayed, so usually you will want participants to be able to enter freely upon connecting. However, for some very formal meetings, it may be appropriate to leave it off.

3. **Entry/exit chimes**. Most platforms will make a "doorbell" type sound when participants enter or leave. These can be very distracting to those already on the call and we generally advise turning them off.

The last thing you want during a critical

moment of a discussion is a doorbell chime indicating someone has left. It makes everyone wonder, "Who just left? I wonder why? Was it something we said?" and now they have lost their place in the conversation. It can also really dampen a crisp opening or closing of a meeting to have chimes interrupting critical comments.

There may be cases where you want to be aware of people entering/existing for privacy reasons or to be sure to acknowledge them and you can either turn these chimes on or you can have someone monitoring the participant list for you. Some platforms also permit these chimes to be heard only by the host.

4. **Record meeting.** One highly valuable capability of web conferencing platforms is their ability to automatically record meetings for playback later. This is useful for participants who may have to miss the meeting or for project managers who want to be sure they have correctly captured all the action items and want to be able to replay. I often listen to missed meetings at 1.5x speed on playback for greater efficiency.

Recordings can generally include not just audio, but screen sharing and video as well, and many platforms now also offer a text transcription. This is fantastic for searching as well as scanning to get a quick overview of the meeting without needing to listen to it in real time. Very often it's worthwhile to turn this feature "on." Just bear in mind that if the meeting is on a sensitive or controversial topic, then the recording is sensitive as well.

Also, most conferencing platforms proactively notify participants that they are being recorded. In my experience most people are fine with this and forget that it's even recording after a few minutes, but it's possible some people may be uncomfortable or may reserve what they say due to the recording. Let participants know that if at any point they feel they want the meeting to go "off the record," the recording can be paused.

5. **Mute participants on arrival.** All conferencing platforms allow participants to mute themselves, but many also allow the organizer to set it so that participants *start* the conference muted and must un-mute themselves to speak. This is most useful in online meetings of more than 20 people when the background noise of so many participants would be overwhelming.

6. **Turn on video by default.** As we have mentioned and will discuss more in a coming chapter, getting participants accustomed to leaving their cameras on during online meetings is a very valuable custom to establish. One way to give people "the hint" about this is to set it so that when they join the conference, their camera turns on automatically.

The downside to this is if the camera turns on before the participant realizes they are "on camera," embarrassing things can occur. However, even if this feature is enabled by the moderator, most software will still ask the user for permission to access their camera upon joining each meeting.

In most cases, we do recommend this setting, but be sure to communicate to participants that it will be enabled. It can be helpful to include this expectation in advance communication, so everyone is equally prepared to be on camera (and not finding themselves to be the odd person out with their camera off.)

7. **Enabling other features you intend to use.** Be sure to take a stroll through your platform settings - it can actually be quite enlightening, especially given features are often being added or updated. Many platforms have optional features such as chat or whiteboards that moderators can enable or disable as they see fit. It can be worthwhile to turn off features you don't plan to use to avoid distraction, and be sure you have turned *on* those you will be utilizing.

During the Engagement chapter of the book, we will discuss the use of many features such as chat and polls to help you determine which features make sense for any given meeting.

Testing & Rehearsal

If you want things to go smoothly, rehearse them in advance. The criticality of a completely polished meeting may vary situationally. If the meeting is for a large group and the stakes are high, it's advisable to do a complete run-through. Use the conferencing software and have all the presenters and facilitator practice their roles and use the real presentation materials. You may even want a small "test audience," to ask questions or participate in any interactive aspects of the presentation.

If it's a smaller or more laid-back affair, all that may be overkill, but it's still wise to be on the conference bridge at least 10 minutes early to be sure everything is working correctly and give yourself time to troubleshoot without "eating into" the scheduled meeting time.

Train your participants that they should show up on time and prepared for online meetings, and that just to be safe it's good to dial in a minute or two early. The first step to doing that is to model that behavior as a leader of those meetings and be ready when they join.

Likewise, understand that many people may need to jump to their next meeting a minute or two before the end of your meeting, so be mindful of ending meetings a tad early to allow for this. In some organizations, it's an accepted rule of engagement to end meetings a few minutes early to allow people a clean start for their next meeting, and you are far better off with a clean ending to the meeting with all attendees still present than a final few minutes where participants are dropping off one by one.

CHAPTER 5

Online Meeting Technology

Online meetings bring together a number of technologies which must work together in order for the experience to be effective.

1. **Online meeting platform (OMP).** The first technology you probably think of is the webinar platform you are utilizing, such as Zoom or Webex.

   This is cloud-based software that connects your meeting participants together and provides a variety of other features which we will discuss below.

2. **Connecting device.** All participants will need to connect to the OMP with a device of some sort, i.e., a laptop or desktop computer, a tablet, phone or a smartphone. Some platforms even have connectivity for wearable devices like Apple Watches or large devices like Smart TVs.

   Furthermore, some platforms can integrate with high-end video conferencing systems, such as Cisco Telepresence or Polycom, often installed in conference rooms of large companies.

3. **Connectivity**. Devices need a wired or wireless connection of some sort (wifi or cellular) to connect to the OMP. Modern conferencing systems that support screen sharing and video work better on high bandwidth connections.

4. **Peripherals**. Your connected device probably has a camera and microphone built into it, however, for some purposes, it's helpful to use higher quality cameras or external microphones or headsets. Depending on your use, other peripherals such as drawing tablets or second monitors can also be beneficial.

Let's take a look at these technology groups one at a time.

Meeting Platform Choice

There are a wide range of web-based platforms that work well for online meetings. These include Zoom, Webex, GoToMeeting, Google Hangouts, and Skype for Business. Most likely, your company already has a platform, and you are more focused on making the most of it rather than trying to select one.

If you *do* need to select a platform, on the book web site ImpactfulOnlineMeetings.com there are links to some helpful guides you can use to compare the features and other characteristics of the competing platforms to find one that best fits your needs.

At our company, we use Zoom for internal use. However, because we work with many clients who have a wide range of different platforms already in place, we have experience with many of the options out there. The good news is that there are many good choices, and many of them have similar features. Naturally, each has something that sets it apart in the market, but the similarities between these platforms— at least the major ones—generally outweigh the differences.

In this book, we will focus on more general guidance that will apply to most platforms rather than talking about any one in particular. If you have questions about how to implement what is discussed here on your specific platform, you can try consulting your platform's documentation or help chat or post your question on the book website, and we will try to help you out.

Connecting Device

You have a wide range of device options for connecting to web conferencing software.

In a pinch, you can join a conference from your smartphone. While we certainly don't recommend it, we have seen many clients join video calls from a phone mounted on their car dashboard while they were driving down the highway.

It's good to know the smartphone option is available; however, it's usually not the best choice as it is harder to see the screen given its size and also more difficult to access conferencing tools like chat while also being able to see what is going on.

Far better is to utilize a laptop or desktop computer with a good-sized screen. Online meetings don't require super-fast computers in order to function well. Normally, any computer manufactured in the last few years that is not a "bottom of the barrel" model will probably work adequately. If you are uncertain, it is best to test the device before it's time to join a critical meeting.

Many online meeting platforms also require you to download software to your device in order to join a meeting. It's wise to ensure this is installed well ahead of time in order to avoid a delay in joining a meeting. Installing the software can take anywhere from thirty seconds to a few minutes, assuming you don't encounter any problems.

Also, take a tour of the interface before the meeting. Features may operate differently and there is often more limited functionality on mobile versions, particularly for "hosts", versus what you may be used to on a laptop, so you'll want to be prepared for this.

And one problem you *may* encounter happens if your device (phone or computer) is "managed" by your company. You may need special permission or an administrator in order to install new software, so again, don't wait until the last minute to discover that the security on your device is blocking you from installing what you need.

Some, but not all, platforms allow you to join a call through a web browser without installing any software. This is a good option if you are blocked on the software install, however the quality is often lower than when using the native software.

Connectivity

In order to have a smooth experience on the web conference, you will need at least moderately fast, reliable connectivity.

If you are having difficulty with connection or audio/video quality, test the speed of your internet connection. You can do this by going to Google and entering "internet speed test" into the search bar and following the instructions.

After a minute or so the test will provide you a numerical measurement of your connection speed measured in either kilobits per second or megabits per second.

Ideally you want to ensure you have at least 1.5 megabits per second (sometimes abbreviated mbps) for both upload and download speed. It takes 1024 kilobits to make a megabit, so if your readings are coming back in kilobits your speed is probably too slow for fully effective web conferencing. At speeds of 600kbps it is certainly possible to have a successful audio connection but you may want to turn off video if you are significantly below that 1.5 megabit level.

Cellular

Cellular 4G networks have become impressively fast and, depending on your location, these can work surprisingly well even with video. But they can also be unreliable and break up in the middle of a call, so they are not preferred and should be avoided if you are presenting or facilitating. Next generation 5G networks are being rolled out by carriers like Verizon in the U.S. and they promise greater reliability; however, they are not yet widely available as of this printing.

Wifi

Wifi connectivity is usually fine if you are reasonably close to the wifi access point and the underlying connection to the internet is solid and fast.

Wired

Of course, the least risky way to connect is via a wired ethernet connection, although in our world today this is less and less common.

Firewalls

Although corporate networks are usually quite fast and reliable, whether via wifi or wired connections, they can also present problems.

It is not uncommon for large enterprises to configure their network to "block" certain brands of web conferencing software because they believe it could pose a security risk. Not being a security expert, I have no point of view on whether this is a real risk; however, we've seen different large companies blocking every major brand of conferencing software between them.

Typically, if you are using your own company's chosen platform this should not be a problem. However, when we have our consulting clients join conference calls that we set up using our Zoom account, it's not uncommon to find they have trouble connecting due to settings on their corporate network. When this occurs, a quickie solution is for them to just join via their smartphone or to use their smartphone's "tethering" feature to allow their laptop or desktop to access 4G using wifi. But this is suboptimal for the reasons mentioned above.

If you are connecting from home or a hotel and having these difficulties, try disconnecting from your company's VPN software so that you will not be limited by your enterprise network restrictions. That may solve the problem; however, it may also block you from accessing other important business tools at the same time.

Telephone

In addition to connecting through the internet, most conferencing systems give you the ability to dial in "the old fashioned way" from a phone line. Often there are both regular and toll-free numbers as well as international numbers to avoid long distance charges.

Also, typically today, many platforms will provide you the dial-in information in a "mobile-friendly" dial-in format in the meeting information, meaning smartphone uses can tap the dial-in from a meeting invite or email and it will dial both the phone number and pause and then dial the meeting ID, so you don't have to key it in.

The format you will typically see will have the phone number without punctuation, followed by several commas, then the meeting passcode and then a # sign. Example: +13126262799,,352355511#.

But joining a remote meeting via "telephone only" is far from optimal as you cannot see any shared screens or videos nor can you access chat, whiteboards, or other tools of the conferencing system. Therefore, doing so should be used only in a situation where there is no better option (or if the call doesn't take advantage of any of those features, but as we'll talk about in coming chapters, the most effective online meetings *do* utilize those features).

Hybrid

One option that is far more workable, however, is a hybrid connection. In this mode, you join the webinar using a computer or other connected device, and you *also* dial in via a phone line.

The benefit of connecting via phone is that very often the audio quality and reliability of a phone line will exceed what you will get from an internet-based connection. No matter how fast your connectivity, web meetings travel through the open internet so there are various factors that are totally outside your control, your company's control, or even the web platform company's control, that can still impact the quality of the connection.

For my most important online meetings, we use this approach to get the benefits of rock-solid phone-based audio as well as the video and screen-sharing capabilities of the web-based platform. The other benefit is that it can also allow for more physical flexibility. If you find you need to step away from the computer momentarily, you can still stay connected to the audio.

The only caveat is that if you join in this way, you need to be sure to mute your computer and turn the volume down as well to avoid feedback, echos, or other interference. Furthermore, when participants join in this way they can appear to others as if they are two different attendees, confusing the count of participants.

That's why it's important, when available, for participants to key in "participant ID" so the system can link your video presence and your audio connection.

Peripherals

There are three types of peripherals most useful for online meetings: headsets, additional monitors, and drawing tablets.

Headsets

The quality of the microphones built into laptops is variable, and some desktops don't even have microphones built in. If you will be participating in or leading online meetings with any regularity, it is highly recommended that you purchase a headset that you plug into your device's "aux" port. In a pinch, the earbuds that come with an older iPhone or other smartphone that isn't using a proprietary adapter can do the trick, but there are better options available. A list of recommended products at different price points is provided on the book website, ImpactfulOnlinePresentations.com.

A good headset will make your voice sound both clearer and richer and will eliminate more of the background noise.

Furthermore, if you are using a laptop and plan to type at all during the meeting (for example to take notes) microphones embedded into laptops amplify typing noise and it can be distracting to those on the call (and make it sound like you are multitasking even if you aren't). This problem is largely eliminated with a headset.

If you are using the strategy described above to use a "regular" telephone for the audio portion of the call, there are still numerous headset options, and you will no doubt prefer that to holding the phone to your ear for an hour or more. Many "cordless" phones have an aux input that is similar to that on computers and older smartphones. It is slightly smaller, but inexpensive adapters are available to make the same headsets work with those phones. Links to these supplies are available on the book website.

We do not recommend using the speakerphone of your mobile or regular phone for your audio option as the audio sound for those listening to you is nearly always lower quality and usually there is more background noise picked up.

If you opt to use a wireless headset, and we know the world is shifting this way, be aware that they vary greatly in sound quality, battery life, and the distance they can be from the audio source. Often, it's the battery life that is the kicker. If you are going to be on back-to-back phone calls, as we are finding ourselves to be more and more, you'll need to be prepared to recharge and use another audio option in the meantime. Today, the only fully reliable bluetooth headsets are at the top of the line (such as Bose). If you want to go Bluetooth to have that convenience, be prepared to invest. It's worth it.

We recommend defaulting to wired headsets, especially if you are leading a session, as most Bluetooth headsets are not yet 100% reliable.

Second Monitors

If you will be frequently participating in online meetings (and especially if you are leading them), it is a great convenience to have an additional LCD monitor. Often, these can be purchased for less than $150.

With a second monitor, you can share your screen on one if you are presenting and use the second screen to see the chat, take notes, or access other applications you may need such as a browser or your calendar without this being seen by meeting participants.

Drawing Tablets

Another useful and inexpensive peripheral if you are going to be leading a lot of online meetings is a drawing tablet. These plug into the USB port on a computer and allow you to much more effectively use the whiteboard tools provided by many conferencing applications because they enable you to draw with a pen stylus. Drawing with a mouse has been compared to trying to sketch with a brick. Touchpads, given their size, really aren't much better. Small tablets with an included stylus can be purchased for as little as $75 and make drawing or annotating slides far easier.

CHAPTER 6

Facilitating & Presenting Effectively

People take their cues from leaders. As someone either facilitating an online meeting or presenting as part of one, you are positioned as a leader. How you behave will have a huge impact on the tone and effectiveness of the overall meeting.

Being a Model

We've described throughout the book some of the behavior you will want from participants—for example, being on time, playing full out, not multitasking, having the right equipment, and coming prepared. There is no more effective way to promote these behaviors than to model them as a leader, and conversely there is no better way to undermine them than to model contrary behavior.

Environment

When leading or participating in an online meeting, take care to ensure your environment is conducive to the best possible experience for yourself and for your colleagues "on the other end."

Noise Free

Find a location free from background noise or likely interruptions. Alert others in your space that you are on a call so they know to avoid loud activities near you. Also, avoid environments that have strong echoes as they will also reduce the quality of your voice on the line, especially if you are using a speaker phone.

Remember to turn off the noises coming from your devices—laptop email and instant messaging and various mobile phone notifications. Hearing regular bloops and swooshes throughout your presentation will significantly decrease participants' ability to focus on you and your message. And while others can be muted, you are the presenter, so you cannot...and the bloops will keep blooping.

Visually Clean and Professional

If you are going to be on camera—and you should be—pay attention to what is behind you in the shot. Ensure the background is neat and not distracting. Consider developing a signal for others in your space to know when you are on a "video call" specifically, so they can be on alert and not race into view by accident.

Alternatively, some tools such as Skype for business will blur the background or allow you to automatically insert a substitute background, hiding the environment around you.

Be Aware of Lighting

Are you ready for your closeup? Yes, I know you are not shooting the next great motion picture, but taking a few basic steps to set up flattering lighting can make you appear more professional. We have a video on the book website at ImpactfulOnlineMeetings.com to help you with this.

Also, avoid very bright areas of the background such as the window on a sunny day, as this may cause your camera to darken the entire image, putting you into shadow.

Dress Professionally

You should consider dressing as you would if you were meeting in person. Cultures and situations vary, but remember that you will be judged by others based on your attire and grooming. Jeans and a sweatshirt might be fine for a meeting of your direct reports, but for the executive call, I suggest dressing in office attire—whatever that means in your industry.

Set up your Computer for Sharing

If you are going to be sharing your screen, close extra open applications, confidential documents, email, or other material you would not want to be accidentally seen.

If you have one of those desktops with 10,000 random icons on it (like me), either clean that up or maximize the presentation screen so the audience will not see that mess.

Also, if you have applications that display "pop-up" notifications on your screen, such as iMessage or Slack, turn them off. You don't want to be in the middle of presenting your PowerPoint and have messages from your spouse about taking the dog to the vet appearing in the corner.

Don't Forget...

Write a PostIt to remind yourself that you (and/or your computer screen) are live BROADCASTING. You *know* what not to do when you are on camera, but remember not to *forget* that you are on camera.

Right Before the Meeting Starts

As a leader of an online meeting, you set the tone right from the beginning.

Be Early

Be on the call five minutes before the scheduled start time so you can make sure everything is working and greet participants as they arrive.

Establish the Mood

Meeting attendees will likely be coming from a wide range of different activities and emotional "spaces" when they arrive. Take control of their mindset and mood by facilitating casual conversation before the official start time.

Don't let it be awkwardly silent or dominated by a side conversation between just a few of the many people on the line. On the book website, we have included a PDF of some suggested "conversation starters," but topics like sports, weather, children, vacation plans, movies or TV shows are good, fun topics.

Music

Consider having some music playing when attendees arrive. Not that awful conference call hold muzak but something to set the mood. Maybe it's rock and roll or lively jazz.

When we do in-person workshops, we make extensive use of music to help influence the mood of participants, and so when we started doing online workshops, we experimented with using it there as well, and it worked great.

To allow the music to be "in" the meeting you need the music on or connected to your laptop *and* you'll need to share your screen. Experiment a bit with this before you start. Also, you'll want to think through the right music for the mood and audience and where you want to start a given song - some songs have long intros.

Sometimes we'll bring up an iTunes "visualization" on the screen we are sharing so there's animation "to the music" when people arrive. It's surprising and signals that this isn't going to be a "boring old" conference call.

Kicking it Off

As the leader, it's your job to call the meeting to order. You should have already been setting an example by modeling the right behavior as well as acting as a host facilitating socialization conversation.

Start on Time

It's tempting to wait for latecomers, but as soon as you start with that pattern then everyone starts showing up a bit later.

If there is the case that a critical person has not yet joined, have someone on point to help ping that person and keep the audience apprised of any reasons for a delayed start, so they understand you respect their time. Keep a close eye on the arriving participants so you start as soon as you are able to.

Energy

Model the energy and focus that you want participants to have. People prefer leaders who are in a peak energy state.

Recap the Purpose

Remind everyone of the purpose, reasons, and activities for the meeting. This can be brief, but take the opportunity to remind them of the benefits of success during the meeting.

You might say, "Today's goal is to finalize the form we will use for the performance management process. This is *critical* because it's a tool that will help facilitate thousands of conversations between employees and their supervisors, and many of those conversations will be turning points in those employees' careers. When we get this right we can really impact employee morale, productivity and reduce attrition." Do you feel how just reading that makes the task sound more exciting than just "finalizing a form?"

Also, remind everyone of the criteria by which we will know whether we are successful at the end of the allotted time. You might say, "Our mission is that by the end of this hour we are all aligned on the final wording of all the questions on the form so it can be sent out."

If it's a small group, check with the audience to be sure they are aligned on the goals, and no matter what the group size, ask if the group is *clear* on the goals.

Rules

In the chapter on "planning," we discussed defining meeting rules. You don't want to start every meeting with a dogmatic reading of the rules, but a quick friendly reminder can be helpful. If this is not a regular meeting or if there are participants who may not be familiar with the rules, then it's worthwhile to review them.

Reviewing the rules doesn't have to be boring. They can be reviewed in a fun, positive way. You don't want to sound like the mean first-grade teacher. Instead, reiterate how they are there to enable the whole group to work together better and that they work!

In addition, if there are any meeting-specific rules because this meeting is out-of-the ordinary in some way, then those should be mentioned.

Permission to Facilitate

If you anticipate that you may need to "move things along" at different points in the session, and if this is not a group you meet with regularly, it's good to remind everyone up front that there's a lot to cover, that discussion is highly valued, but at the same time it's your job to watch the clock. Let them know that if the group's ability to complete all the objectives is at risk, that you will ask to move to the next topic and deal with any outstanding items offline.

Getting the "permission" of the group on that point in advance can make it easier to deal with if/when it comes up.

Introductions

Introductions are clearly necessary when the people at a meeting don't all know each other.

When facilitating introductions, it's important to give specific directions as to what they are being asked to speak to, and ideally put them on a slide on the screen. This is because some people will take the "introduction" opportunity to provide more detail than you may want at this point in the meeting.

A example set of instructions for introductions are, for example, to tell the group:

1. Your name
2. Your department
3. Your role
4. Something most people don't know about you (a brief fun fact)

This last item is meant to help participants get to know each other a bit better beyond "name, rank and serial number."

According to Slack's *Ultimate Guide to Remote Meetings,* "One study found that workers who shared a funny or embarrassing story about themselves with their team produced 26% more ideas in brainstorming sessions than workers who didn't."

And if participants already know each other pretty well, then consider doing a personal-professional check-in at the beginning of each meeting. Encourage team members to give a 60 seconds or less verbal "tweet" on what the headline in their life is right now.

When facilitating introductions, work from a list of who is on the line and call on people one at a time to speak. While this is less "organic," it helps avoid the classic uncertainty on online calls of "who should go next," since there is no way to "go around the table."

If you are facilitating a meeting of more than 10-12 people, these strategies of having everyone on the call introduce themselves start to become impractical as you could spend half the meeting just on introductions.

When that occurs, you can ask everyone to type their introduction into the chat. That gives everyone the feeling of having introduced themselves (to some degree) and allows participants to scan the full set in much less time than verbal intros would take.

Or if much of the group know each other but there are a few new faces, you might just want to ask those new people to do the intro.

Muting Noisy Participants

One of the great nuisances of online meetings is when a participant has background noise and hasn't muted their phone. Meeting organizers are constantly having to stop and say, "Can whoever has background noise please mute your phone?" That causes everyone on the call to shift their focus to whether their phone is muted and lose their stream of thought as it relates to the presentation or discussion. Don't do it that way.

Here's an alternative. Most conferencing software allows moderators to mute anyone on the call. You have been granted mighty powers, use them! What is most practical is to have someone *other* than the presenter or facilitator assigned to keep an eye (or an ear) out for background noise and mute offenders. When a participant is muted, you can send them a text on the conference platform letting them know that due to background noise you muted their line. They can still "unmute" themselves if they wish to speak.

Now you may be wondering, how will I know *which participant is causing the background noise?* On most conferencing platforms, if you look at the list of participants, there will be some type of indication if there is sound coming from their line. It may be a tiny animated bar graph or a pulsing circle, but there is usually some indicator. Naturally, the person who is speaking at the moment will show this kind of activity, but look for *other* participants who are not the speaker and where the movement of the sound indicator is consistent with the volume changes in the background noise. This is your culprit.

Presenting Effectively

When presenting during an online meeting, there are a number of things you can do to maximize your effectiveness.

Story

People pay attention to stories. They tend to snooze when people start talking in bullet points (and especially reading bullet points out loud), so try to find a way to make your content into a story or series of stories.

Brevity

Look to the meeting outcomes to determine what the audience really *needs* to know, and only cover that. Give the high level. Better to have time for questions and go into detail where the audience needs it.

Tone of Voice

Practice varying your tone of voice—pitch, rhythm and volume—and it will make your presentations more interesting to listen to. You can't really think much about this *while* presenting, but, if you practice it offline, it will increase your vocal expressiveness even when you aren't thinking about it.

Body Language

Use your body language to help tell your story if you are on camera. And don't forget to smile!

Using the Camera

One way to create additional drama during online presentations is to vary your distance from the camera.

In a TV broadcast the camera will shift from closer shots to wider shots as the anchor or commentator goes along, mainly just for variety.

You can mimic this subtly. Slide or even lean back a bit and you will get smaller in the frame and show more of the background, lean forward for more dramatic effect. Variety is one of the things that keeps presentations interesting.

Also remember that when you are looking into or near the camera, it will appear to the audience that you are looking at them. But if you have a large monitor and, for example, the audience member video is at the bottom and you look at that, it may appear you're looking below the audience. The best thing to do is to place the video of the audience as close as possible to the top of your screen where the camera is so, when you are looking at their video, it looks to them like you are looking at *them*.

Handoffs Between Presenters

Practice to make handoffs between presenters smooth. Be sure you know who is going next and presenters are clear on the order so they are not surprised.

When it's your turn, be ready and turn mute off a few seconds before the baton gets passed to you.

Don't be the person who is silent for the first 15 seconds and then comes on and says, "Doh! I forgot I was on mute." We've all done it, and now it's been done *too many times*. It's not cute anymore.

Reading your Audience

One of the benefits you lose when you move from in-person to online meetings is the ability to easily "read the room"—to gauge, by assessing the audience's reactions, how you're doing as you present.

As a presenter it is *essential* that you are getting feedback from your audience. It's very awkward when presenters finally stop and ask, "Are you guys still there?" but it happens all the time. Don't be that guy (or gal). Instead, build natural feedback into your presentation, and if necessary quickly train your audience on how to be responsive in this media. Here are a few alternatives:

Video

As we will continue to reiterate, creating a webinar culture where participants turn on their cameras is the number one best way to get more feedback. While it's not as good as being in the room where you can observe more of their body language, you can still see a lot from facial expressions and body position.

Once you have participants turning on their cameras, you want to be sure that, as a presenter, you are looking at your audience, and not filling your only screen up with your slides and robbing yourself of the chance to actually *see* those facial expressions.

Ideally, you have two monitors as described previously. In that case, use one for the video component and the other for your slides. Alternatively, bring your slides up in a smaller window and only share that window with the audience, and then use the remainder of your screen for the video images of the audience.

Chat

You can get feedback by asking your audience to enter something into the chat. Ask a question like, "What do *you* think is the most important aspect of our customer service?" and ask all in attendance to quickly go to their chat and enter a one- to two- word answer. You then not only know they are "still there," but you are engaging with them and getting some feedback. You are having a dialog with your audience.

Group Verbal Feedback

Another approach that can work extremely well but requires two minutes of training for the audience is to ask for group verbal feedback.

Before you begin speaking, let them know how you will be asking the questions and that when you do, they are to go off mute and speak simultaneously. It will sound like a big mess, but everyone will get a sense of the "energy" of the full group on the phone (it can be startling) and you still can probably hear if, for example, everyone is saying "yes" or everyone is saying "no" or if it's a mix.

Handling Questions and Discussion

As a presenter or facilitator, at one point you will want to ask questions of the group and facilitate discussion.

Discussion in online meetings requires more active facilitation than it usually requires in small to medium-sized in-person meetings.

This is because of the potentially awkward problem on conference calls of "who will speak next." This is particularly problematic in sessions of over ten people.

Without management, participants tend to interrupt each other or wait until someone has finished and try to "jump in" as quickly as possible to get in before someone else starts talking. While this has the advantage of keeping people "on their toes," it substantially disadvantages less extroverted team members and is generally a somewhat stressful experience. As we mentioned in the introductory chapters, keeping participants' mindsets positive and open is a key to success, and that is undermined by the competition for speaking that happens on crowded web meetings.

One basic way for somewhat smaller, more intimate meetings with more active discussion is to have people on video and have them raise their hands or a finger to indicate they want to speak. This is visible to all participants and can help people be more brief in their comments if they know others have comments to share as well. Using this technique does require the facilitator to scroll through the video streams to keep an eye out for those with their hands raised however.

Also, some platforms now have a specific Q&A feature which allows questions to be posted and also allow other participants to "Like" a question if they have the same one. This moves the popular questions to the top to help you address what's important to the group. It also allows responses to be posted by facilitators and participants, which can be helpful.

When this Q&A feature is not available, the best alternative we've found, particularly for larger meetings, is a queuing system using chat. You can either simply ask people to type into the chat "I have a question" or something similar mentioning their topic and wait to be recognized by the facilitator.

This also allows the facilitator to see how many people wish to comment (as can everyone) and, ideally, about which topics. Therefore, the facilitator can better orchestrate sequencing of speakers and topics and how long people will have to speak.

Furthermore, if some participants have dominated discussion and others haven't had much chance to speak, the facilitator can give preference to those who are "in line" but have had less speaking time.

Some conferencing systems also have a "raise my hand" button, which functions similarly and lets the facilitator know that person would like to be recognized.

Another variation on the chat approach is to ask participants to actually put their comments or questions themselves right into the chat. The advantage of that is you might find that half of the people are asking some variation of the same question and then most likely that topic would be prioritized for discussion. Another benefit of this method is that any questions or comments that there isn't time to cover are still recorded for further follow-up after the meeting.

If you choose to use this method, it's good to do a quick practice round before you use it with the group for the first time. Explain how it works and then ask a silly question like, "Who was the best Beatle?" (Correct answer: Ringo) and let people type their answers and get a sense of where the group is coming from. For a Millennial audience, you can substitute, "Who was the best Ninja Turtle?" (Correct answer: Michelangelo). After they've done it once in fun, the group will be warmed up to do it for the real content.

For any meeting with a sizable audience using tools that take input from the audience, we recommend having another person help to manage the incoming content so the facilitator can be engaged in managing the discussion vs trying to find the next speaker and ignoring the person talking. This helper can also respond to some questions in written form to leave more discussion time for other questions.

But What If Nobody Says Anything?

While sometimes you'll have to work hard to manage all the people that want to speak, at other times you may ask for questions or comments and nobody says anything (or raises their hand in the chat, if you are using that system). What do you do then?

First of all, just wait. A bit of silence on a call is ok and even encouraged, in order to help pull people out of their shells.

It might take a moment for people to process the question, decide what to say, and either go off mute or type it into the chat. Sometimes those few seconds can seem like hours, but stay confident.

Even if nobody seems to be jumping to answer, it's ok to give it another ten seconds. Most likely by then someone will have collected their thoughts and will jump in. And then usually once someone sees "the water's fine," you will get more participation.

In the unlikely event that should fail, you can be ready with some specific questions, and you may want to use the chat for those. Ask the group about some specific aspect of the topic and see where people's heads are at, and then pick someone who entered a response in the chat and ask them to elaborate.

Knowing Who is Speaking

One challenge of the experience of being on an online meeting is knowing who is speaking at any given moment. Many conferencing platforms help this by showing the name of the speaker if they've joined by computer and entered their name, but this may not always be noticed by participants and generally doesn't work for any that are dialed in. Therefore, it's a good practice to train those on large calls to start any questions or comments by identifying who is speaking.

If they forget, at a suitable pause in their comments it's good to clarify for the group who is speaking or to ask the speaker to clarify it.

Spiraling Discussions, Filibusters and Other Problems Managing Discussion

Once you get people talking, you may find the conversation gets animated, which is a positive step, but that can also present challenges with staying on your agenda.

It's important when planning a meeting to factor in time for discussion, but some discussions can seem like they would go on indefinitely.

This is exacerbated in the online world because in an in-person meeting if a conversation is going too long there may be nonverbal cues from other participants that those continuing the discussion can read and it may well give them the hint that the group doesn't want the conversation to keep using meeting time. While that is not sure-fire when in-person, it's absent in calls without video, and its effectiveness is reduced even in video calls since nonverbal cues are more muted when you are looking at postage-stamp sized videos of your colleagues.

If you let conversations keep going too long, you frustrate your other participants (impairing their mindsets) and you may not be able to achieve all the meeting objectives because you will have used too much time on discussion. So it's the job of the facilitator to move things along. Here are several tactics:

Acknowledge the Importance of the Topic

If you need to "wrap it up" on a given topic even though the group hasn't come to consensus or someone's concern has not been fully addressed, it's good to start by acknowledging the validity of the issue. Most issues have at least *some* level of validity even if you don't agree with the person's overall point. You might say, "We really haven't figured out a solution to Bill's concern that allowing customers to put paper in the photocopiers we sell is killing trees, but there's no question that the environment is a very important topic, and I appreciate that he's raised the issue…"

Remind Them of the Permission They Gave You

You can then remind the group that you have the unenviable job of being the timekeeper of the meeting and that in the interest of everyone's shared goal of achieving the meeting objectives, you'd like to give two more minutes (or some period of time) remaining to round out discussion on the topic and then move any further discussion outside of the session.

Focus Them on the Meeting Objectives

Another way to try to shortcut what might appear to be an out of control conversation is to refocus participants on the meeting objectives that were defined at the start of the session. Ask the question, "Is resolving this issue necessary in order for us to achieve our objectives?"

It may be that some feel that it *is*, but at least you have the possibility that the majority of the group feels that the objectives can be achieved even if this issue is *not* resolved, in which case it justifies "moving on" for now.

If enough people feel that the issue *is* truly critical, then it's ok to ask, "Is it important enough that we should keep spending time on it even if that means we may not achieve some of the other goals we set for this hour?" The group may feel that, no, the other goals are more important, *or* they may feel the issue is *so* important that it trumps the other goals.

If so, it might be time to be flexible as a facilitator and focus on the topic even if it crowds out other planned parts of the agenda.

In that case, you can support the group by trying to help them focus. You might say, "Well, we have 20 minutes left of this meeting. What could we get done on this issue in the next 20 minutes that would move the ball forward?"

The group may decide they can't resolve the issue but can at least develop a strategy to gather the information after the meeting that will enable the matter to be solved or define whatever activities will be practical within the remaining meeting time.

You can then use the last couple of minutes of the meeting to develop a plan to address the items on the agenda that got "bumped" for this more important issue. Perhaps a follow-up meeting is warranted.

CHAPTER 7

Audience Engagement and Interaction

As we said early in the book, one of the five components for a successful online meeting is participant *engagement*. You want people on the edge of their seats, not watching the clock or checking their email.

We've already talked about some techniques to make presentations more effective as well as to make sure participants know the purpose of the meeting and why it's so important. These practices will help keep people focused. But the number one method to keep people focused is to give them a role so they cannot hide; they are not an "audience;" they are active participants.

In an in-person meeting, all participants can see all the other participants and so merely by their body language and reactions they have at least a minimal "role" in the meeting.

While, of course, some people still "tune out" in an in-person meeting, online meetings are far, far easier to tune out from; therefore, it's even more critical that you have a solid strategy for engagement.

And just to be totally clear, what do we mean by engagement? We mean that the participants are *doing* something. They are not merely passive listeners or watchers of the webinar, but they have an active role.

When people have an active role they are far, far more attentive, as in the story I told earlier when I kept score at my daughter's basketball game. That was one tactic we already discussed to get people engaged: give them a role such as taking notes, monitoring the chat log for audience questions, or muting people with background noise. Now let's look at some *other* techniques for keeping people engaged:

Turn on Video

As has been mentioned repeatedly, encouraging or even requiring participants to turn on their video cameras is valuable for many reasons. One reason is that it immediately makes them more engaged because they can be *seen*; therefore their reactions are part of "the show" versus something private.

Furthermore, one of the greatest obstacles to audience engagement is multi-tasking. Once they start checking their Instagram, not only are they not actively engaged with the meeting, they probably aren't even listening. When the cameras are "on," people are less likely to multitask freely because they can be seen by others.

Yes, participants will complain at first. We've seen this with many clients. Not to stereotype, but the women will say, "I thought the benefit of telecommuting is that I didn't have to do my hair and makeup!" The guys will say, "Hey man, I haven't even showered," or "I just did my workout; don't make me turn the camera on!"

Tough. If the meeting is worthwhile, it's worth committing to. They'll still see many other benefits of working at home, for example: avoiding their commute, having homemade lunch with their spouse, tossing in a load of laundry between calls, or being able to be home when their kids get off the school bus.

By the way, leaving video on during online meetings is the standard policy at Google. If it's good enough for Google, maybe your team can get used to it?

And you know what? They will. What we've seen happen over and over is that when you exert some pressure and yes, maybe force people a bit to get those cameras on, and then everyone is doing it, people actually like it. Once they accept the slight inconvenience of not being able to leave their hair in a scrunchie or needing to shave (and we use both of these examples gender-neutrally), they realize it's a much better experience to speak to people eye to eye.

Polls

Most online meeting platforms have the ability for the host to put a multiple-choice poll out to all attendees and then show a graph of participant responses. This can be a great, quick way to both keep people engaged and check where there is consensus or dissent on key issues without needing to hear individually from everyone.

The polls generally need to be prepared in advance, so bear that in mind. Alternatively, if you have people in "support roles," as we have recommended, if an important issue comes up spontaneously that you want to poll, send a private text to the person "on point" to support presentation needs and ask them to quickly create the poll. It should only take 1-2 minutes, and ask them to text you back when it's ready. Keep the discussion going while you wait and then when you get the message that the poll is ready, let the group know you'd like to poll them on the topic and that will be the cue for your support person to put the poll up on the screen. You will look like a magician since you "just happened," to have a poll ready to go on the very topic that came up spontaneously on the call. It's good if your participants think you are "all-knowing," then they are less likely to try to multitask without being noticed.

By the way, if your conferencing platform doesn't have a polling feature there are many on the web. You can just send a group message out with the url and ask participants to click it to access the poll and then share your screen with the results as they come in. Almost as easy. We've put a list of some recommended ones on the book website ImpactfulOnlineMeetings.com.

Chat Questions

Similar to the poll mentioned above is the technique we discussed earlier to throw a question out to the group and have them type their free-response answers into the chat stream.

Play a Game

We sometimes play a "fun facts" game by having each participant send a private chat message to the facilitator with a "fun fact" about their past that others on the call wouldn't be likely to know.

For example, the "fun fact" that I often use is that when I was in college I represented NYU on the television game show "Win, Lose or Draw!"

I lost.

Anyway, then between each topic of the meeting, the host can read off one or two "fun facts" and ask the audience to guess who they refer to, either via chat or verbally if the group is small enough.

Another format involves virtual breakout groups, where you pin different groups against each other in a competition. For example, an uplifting game is to have each breakout group take just 5 minutes to brainstorm the most successes or achievements they can think of from the past year and then have them read them out - giving points for most and for the most that are unique.

Other quick games involve asking a question and having people respond in chat with their guess or response - movie trivia, celebrity trivia, most remote dial-in location from the rest of the group, best vacation, best celebrity experience, most impressive athletic feat, or any other provocative and fun topic you can quiz people about. Yes, some of these are subjective, but in those cases you can get the group to weigh in with cheering for their favorite response.

Get Everyone Involved

Seek to involve as many people as possible in having an active role in the meeting, for example by assigning many people with presentation roles.

Sometimes we even do this "on the spot." For example, at a meeting to review selected customer feedback that had been received on a product, we put the feedback on a slide, picked three participants, and asked them to alternate between reading the 15 to 20 lines of feedback to the group. No rehearsal needed.

As we discussed earlier, there are various other roles outside that of presenter which can be divided up to others in the meeting. This will keep them on their toes and listening instead of being lured away by their backlog of emails.

Collaborate on a Deliverable

Another way to create engagement is to use a cloud collaboration platform such as Google Drive, Microsoft 365, or Sharepoint to enable participants to collaborate on a deliverable simultaneously.

For example, you are probably familiar with a SWOT analysis in which a slide is broken into four quadrants meant to be filled with a company or product's **S**trengths, **W**eaknesses, **O**pportunities, and **T**hreats.

Instead of *presenting* a completed SWOT to your meeting participants, consider putting a link to a blank SWOT slide in Google Slides and asking them all to simultaneously work on filling it in. In under two minutes you will have a completed SWOT that represents the collaborative efforts of the group. With a very large group you can consider directing people to different questions or different pages of the same questions to have fewer people trying to type into the same place.

You could then ask different members that participated to explain items they added to the slide. Or you can pick different people to each read out different sets of responses from the group.

Of course, this can be done with a wide range of other types of documents: idea lists, project plans, lists of competitors, etc. You'll be amazed at the amount and quality of information that can be gathered in a very short time.

Virtual Breakout Groups

In most meetings of more than eight people, usually most of the talking is done by just five to seven participants, no matter how many are present. This is one reason why during live workshops we often break larger groups into breakout teams, so they can come up with ideas, work on prioritization, action planning—whatever the work is—in smaller groups and then come back to the larger group and report on the work they did. It gives more people the opportunity to participate.

It also helps serve as a way to cultivate relationships across a larger group. And, another great benefit is that you can have multiple groups working simultaneously on different topics for greater productivity.

When we use breakouts in workshops, we give each team clear instructions for the work they are to do (in writing) and then usually give them a small amount of time to do it, like 20 to 40 minutes. A compressed time frame forces the group to organize quickly, get to work, and focus on progress, not process or perfection.

We've been amazed over the years that sometimes when clear instructions, a small team, and a tight timeframe are combined like that, you get work done in a half hour that might have taken days, weeks or months if done "the usual way."

The good news is that several of the major online meeting platforms including Zoom and WebEx now offer breakouts,with Zoom offering the ability to create up to 50 breakout rooms

Managing Group Assignments

Features vary between platforms, but generally there are two ways to assign participants to groups. You can either assign participants to groups or you can have the system make random assignments. In a situation like the SWOT exercise above where random groups would be fine, the random option is great and it's easy.

However, when you know that you need certain people to be with other people or you need a facilitation team member in each group, you'll want to pre-think the group assignments. One catch about pre-thinking the groups lists is that you need to be prepared for the case where some participants don't show up and you have to rejigger your teams on the fly. This can be okay with just a few breakout groups, but it can become unwieldy with a larger number of groups and participants.

In the Breakout

When it's time to go to breakouts, the host pushes a button and like magic the participants are transported into breakout channels where each can only hear and see the other people on their breakout team. Within a team they can see video and screen share just like the larger meeting, but each is independent, like its own meeting.

The host, however, can move back and forth between the breakout rooms.

The host can push messages to the groups, such as giving them a two-minute warning or letting them know we're adding five more minutes to the allotted time, or any other useful information. In addition, breakout participants can hit the "Ask for Help" button, and the host will be notified that you need assistance and prompted to join your breakout room.

There is also a time clock that is set for the designated breakout time, so if your breakouts are set to close automatically at a certain time, participants can pace themselves properly (as long as they actually notice the clock.)

Capturing and Sharing Virtual Breakout Content

Very often, the way we will use these capabilities is to break a larger group into small groups of no more than five to eight people each, give each group an assignment and a Google Slides or Google Doc template to work on, and leave them to their own devices. They will generally self-organize, which we prefer. Someone will share their screen, and the group will start discussing and collaborating on a deliverable.

Of course, what works best if it's possible is that all participants have access to the same collaboration tool platform. This way it's as if all participants are walking up to the whiteboard with their own marker to post their comments.

If it's the case where either company firewalls are blocking tool access or too many people are coming from too many companies that you can't count on all the participants being able to access that common tool, a secondary option is to have facilitator/scribes. With this option, which we've used successfully on numerous occasions, you use assigned groups and place a person who does have access to the tool in each of the breakouts. In this case, that facilitator/scribe guides the discussion, while sharing their screen, and captures what the breakout group participants are saying, and the participants are watching the facilitator/scribe populate the document in real time.

When building an exercise, consider how you'll have the groups boil down their mass of brainstormed output into something that can be reported out in a brief time to the large group.

Coming Back Together
As the tight time allocation ticks away, we can visit each breakout group as well as the documents being populated by each one to see how they are doing, and

we can push a message to remind them how much time they have left. When time is up, we give them a few more minutes just to be charitable and then we push the magic button and everyone is instantly rejoined into one meeting.

Then, each team can have one member walk the larger group through the report out slides the team worked on and share their thinking and progress.

We recommend you have each of the breakout groups decide on the presenter(s) before coming back to the big group or you'll likely end up with dead air as everyone waits to see who will volunteer to present.

Summary

Audience engagement is absolutely critical to maximizing the effectiveness of your online meetings.

The material covered in this chapter should give you a large enough toolbox of techniques to keep your participants highly engaged. However, we will post some additional techniques on the book website ImpactfulOnlineMeetings.com if you'd like to check that out as well.

CHAPTER 8

Meeting Closing and Follow Ups

Ending the Meeting

Be sure to leave time in your agenda for at least a two minute "ending" to the online meeting. This creates a polished completion. As part of the ending, you want to do several things.

First, remind everyone what the objectives of the meeting were, and measure progress against the objectives. Hopefully, they are all accomplished, and you can celebrate victory. If the team fell short, indicate what the plan is to address the remainder.

Thank the participants and especially anyone who presented or made a particularly big contribution and ask the rest of the group to thank them as well. Applause is perfectly appropriate.

Action Items

Recap any action items or commitments made during the meeting, who has "taken point" on them, and what the deadlines are.

Notes

Make sure it's clear what is going to happen to any notes taken at the meetings—when will they be completed and how will they be made available?

Meeting Content

Consider in advance how you want to respond to requests to send out the content that was presented. Maybe you'll be posting it in a place where all can access it, or you might be emailing it. Other times you may decide not to distribute it because it's confidential and/or sensitive in some way and you don't want it circulating around. Whatever the case, have the answer ready for your audience..

Feedback Surveys

Consider sending out periodic post-meeting surveys using SurveyMonkey or a similar tool to get a gauge (anonymously if necessary) of participants' experience. Combine these insights to improve future meetings.

CHAPTER 9

Conclusion

Online meetings can be a powerful method of enabling collaborative work. Their many benefits, from location independence to easy screen sharing to recordings with transcriptions, can have a significant impact when used effectively.

While web meetings are not right for all occasions, they are appropriate substitutes for in-person meetings in 75%+ of meeting occasions.

Meeting in the virtual world does come with challenges, but there are also solutions to most of those challenges as outlined in this book. If you combine the powerful and unique benefits of online meetings with the techniques to overcome their potential downsides we've covered here, you have a combination that has the potential to move the needle for your business.

As we said at the start of the book, meetings are the heartbeat of your business. It's where your people get critical information, where ideas are generated, and where important decisions are made. You owe it to yourself and your business to make sure all your meetings, including the increasing percentage of them that are "online," are the best that they can be.

We hope this book has been helpful to you in that endeavor. Remember, there are numerous additional resources to support you and your colleagues in maximizing online meetings on the book website at ImpactfulOnlineMeetings.com. This includes an invaluable pre-flight checklist of the 10 things you must verify before beginning any online meeting.

Also on the website are descriptions of some of the training courses we offer to turn executives and managers into online meeting rock stars.

We hope to see you there!